A Self Expression Of
My Emotions

Nadine Miller-Campbell

WESTBOW°
PRESS
A DIVISION OF THOMAS NELSON
& ZONDERVAN

Scripture taken from the King James Version of the Bible.

Scripture taken from the Holy Bible, NEW INTERNATIONAL VERSION®. Copyright © 1973, 1978, 1984 by Biblica, Inc. All rights reserved worldwide. Used by permission. NEW INTERNATIONAL VERSION® and NIV® are registered trademarks of Biblica, Inc. Use of either trademark for the offering of goods or services requires the prior written consent of Biblica US, Inc.

WestBow Press books may be ordered through booksellers or by contacting:

WestBow Press
A Division of Thomas Nelson & Zondervan
1663 Liberty Drive
Bloomington, IN 47403
www.westbowpress.com
1 (866) 928-1240

Because of the dynamic nature of the Internet, any web addresses or links contained in this book may have changed since publication and may no longer be valid. The views expressed in this work are solely those of the author and do not necessarily reflect the views of the publisher, and the publisher hereby disclaims any responsibility for them.

Any people depicted in stock imagery provided by Thinkstock are models, and such images are being used for illustrative purposes only.
Certain stock imagery © Thinkstock.

ISBN: 978-1-4497-1465-9 (sc)
ISBN: 978-1-4497-1466-6 (e)

Library of Congress Control Number: 2011924989

Print information available on the last page.

WestBow Press rev. date: 4/15/2015

To God be the glory for continuously turning my dreams and desires into reality, and using every part of my life to glorify himself.

To all the people who contributed to the completion of this book. I thank you. In particular, my husband, my mom, my dad Classford Miller (Roy), and my sisters (Debbie, Kim-Marie, and Diana) who have been my constant help, and supporters throughout the compilation of this book. Thank you for celebrating every little victory and accomplished poem.

To Debbie Miller-Curtis, Kerry-Ann Ellington-Robinson, Kay-ann Mighty Brown, Jodi Masters, Dr. Saraswathi Lakshmanan, and Tracy-Ann Vujic for all your encouragements, feedbacks, and editing skills.

To my mother Joyice White and my high school teacher Miss Francis for teaching literature and poems with such joy and enthusiasm, that I fell head over heels in love.

Last, but not least, all the Pastors and spiritual leaders, who have taught, prayed and prophesied God's word and will over my life. I couldn't have learned this much or gotten this far without you. I have matured so much since I started writing this book, and the pages of this book will testify to the remarkable changes.

Prayer

Dear Lord,

Helps us to get through today

Show us the way

We need to hear from you

We need to know you care

We are in dreadful fear

Lord, help us please

We are in serious need

Crime and violence are on a never ending spree

While, Government are expanding

Cemeteries and penitentiaries

Children are having babies

Poverty is on the increase

Too many mouths to feed

The more money we get

The more we seems to need

What is this? Is it greed?

I thought education was the solution

Everyone in school

Where are the jobs for the intellects?

Over qualified and joining the unemployment line.

What is wrong, and how can we be a part of the solution?

It is hard to survive

It is hard to stay alive

It is hard to find our daily bread

People have become cold and mean

Strife and disunity have crept into our communities

The togetherness that builds strength and unity has been stolen by the enemy

If we can't get along

Then, how will we come up with a plan

Much more a solution

Lord can you help us, please?

We are only human

I am not pointing fingers

I am reaching out my hand

I am looking up to heaven

To God, he is the ultimate one

He is the maker of all men

He is the creator of this land

Lord you are the only one

Capable of fixing this devastation

My God and My Guide

You are the difference in my life

You have right the wrong

You are the compass of my life

Through the struggles and the trials, you have always been my guide

Some days it gets dark and lonely, and I have completely lost sight

But I know you are here, the only pure light

When I have drifted, and somehow have lost my way

The Holy Spirit, who lives within, guides me each and every day

Draw me closer to you Jesus, for that's where I want to stay

Surrounded by your glory, covered by your grace

Consumed by your presence is my ideal place

Make me eat the bread of life, and drink your living water

Satisfy my soul, and bring my searching to an end.

A Friend's Love

A friend that is always with me,

A friend that never leaves

He never gets tired, he never gets weary

He has my back; why should I worry?

I can't hide anything from him

He knows everything

But still he loves me unconditionally

I can never disappoint him; He is all knowing

Nothing takes him by surprise

He hardly ever gets upset, and he never stays angry

He calls me his friend, and I am glad he chose me

It's not about what he can give, but what He has already done for me

He is God the Father, the giver of life, and the Redeemer

He is worthy

Sometimes I can't even comprehend it

I am in awe, with the way he loves me

Even when I make a mess

Even when I have done wrong

He still loves me

How could anyone be this kind?

I didn't earn his love, and I can't stop it

He loves me unconditionally

A love like this is hard to find

I try to make myself worthy of his love

But, He is not interested in my performance

He is interested in my heart
Every time I try, it never adds up
If I make a million mistakes
He still does not change
He is helping me to see that it is not about me
It's just who he is, and he cannot change
His name is Jesus Christ
He gave his life for me
He died to save me
His love is not partial
He loves us all the same
You can accept it
You can reject it
I choose to accept it
It would be unwise to reject a love like this

Willingly Purposed

Cleanse my ways oh Lord!
Let my heart be free
Free from all hidden faults
Free to praise you
For unto you, all praises are due
Unto you be honor and glory
Cleans my ways oh Lord!
Let the glory of your face shine on me
Let your Holy Spirit lead me
Let me know the plans you have for me
Only then, will I be fulfilling my purpose
The right purpose of my being
Praise be to God
He has created me for his purpose and pleasure only.

HOLY!

Out of my mouth, I cry Holy! Holy! Holy!
The Lord God Almighty is holy!
He is, indeed worthy of our praises
He created the universe, and beyond what our eyes can see
The earth and the sky testify
From mountains on high to valleys far beneath
The rivers, lakes, and seas
The deserts, wilderness, forest, and fields
The flowers and the trees
Creatures of all kind, great and small
He created them all
People everywhere, all greed and kind
He is the creator of all mankind
They all testify to His marvelous work
Each morning is filled with new love and mercies
His love and kindness are overflowing like a fountain
He is LORD over all
He is the LORD ALMIGHTY
Jesus, you are holy!

Journey of Discoveries

This particular journey was one that thrust me right into that, which God had prepared for me

He gave me a word that unlock the mystery of these plans that he had for me

I was excited to begin this new journey.

On this journey, I have discovered the real meaning of grace

I have found unmerited favor

I have learned how to tap into a higher source

I have discovered God, his love, and his glory

Grace is a beautiful thing, and his love covers all my sins

His love covers all, and it changes everything

On my journey of discovery, I have stumbled upon a few things

Such as: if I can just love, love unselfishly

It brings a deeper satisfaction, which surpasses my expectations

A new year has started; a new day has dawned

Reminiscing, I realize how much I have gained

And how bless I became

I bought a house, started my family, and fulfilled my goal of pursuing a higher education

Nevertheless, I have discovered that in all my uprisings

And in all my gaining and my success

It wasn't my works or my doing

It was God's; his blessings

I have learned that I can't please God, without faith

It was very evident that my war was not with flesh, but against spirits and principalities

I have discovered the wisdom of God, when I truly started fearing him

And in doing so I realize, the battle is not mine, but it is the Lord's

I have discovered that anyone can, and should give God praise

It is just acknowledging where your help comes from, and what he has done

But I have also discovered how to worship, which is a higher level of praise

It means to admire, adore, and appreciate

It has nothing to do with what I have done

But everything to do with who He is

However, on this journey, my greatest discovery was and is

Discovering a God, the only true God, who has created me

Personally

Just for me, just for me
Jesus I know you are here and you care
Just for me, yes he is here for me
There are angels that are standing guard
Just for me, he is always watching over me
You gave me a beautiful family
And a husband that loves me
Lord you are my one and only
Lord you prepared a table before me, so that all can see
You are always providing for me
Just for me, just for me
Through each and everything life throws at me
Jesus you are there, holding me
He is the reason for my sanity
God is here, and he holds it together for me
Jesus never leaves me
He is a friend to the lonely
Just for me, his presence fills me
I am marveled at the thought, that a God, so big
In a world this vast, knows me personally
He created me just like him
He eagerly awaits every morning for me to talk to him
He waits patiently for me, just for me

We Have You

We have you Lord; we have you
You are the Christ our living sacrifice
We have you, yes we have you
You came and died
You paid the price
You carried my pain, and you knew my shame
You took my place
We have you; we have you
You are the Christ, the living sacrifice
And we have you
We are more than conquerors
We are who we are because we have him

We can do all things through him who gives us strength
We have you
We can sing our songs because we have you
We can do our dance because we have you
You rose again, and we have you
You're coming back for your chosen few
And we have you
Live for him, who dies for you
We have you, yes we have you

It Has Always Been GOD

It has always been God
It has always been God
He kept me strong when everything was going wrong.
He held me close
When everyone had let go
He was my friend when I was all alone
There were days that were unbearable
There were times I thought I would lose my mind
There were nights I couldn't sleep
But I knew someone, somewhere was praying for me
God intervened; He kept me strong
It has always been God
I had my portion of bad luck and bad decisions
That left me broken and empty
Helpless and lonely, but God pull me through
God has always been there
He is my constant help, and my only defense
He watches over my soul, and he is in full control

The Seen and the Unseen

The things I see are just as real as the things I feel

I see the goodness of the Lord all around me

I see the miracles he has performed

And the gentle way he is leading me

I see the numerous ways he has shown his love to me

I have also experienced his mercies

I have seen the way he unfolds the day

I can see the sun, and I can see the rain

I can't see the wind, or whence it came

But it is just as real

I can't see love, but I can feel it

I can't see God because no man has ever seen him, but his presence is felt by many

I can't see pain, but I know it's there because I feel it

The things that are unseen are just as real as the things that I have seen

God Meet Me In Between

I know you are there, I know that you care
I know you are real because I can feel you near
The earth belongs to you and everything within
Even though I am aware of this, I often struggle with a few things
I never seem to love enough
Work enough
Listening enough or laugh enough
Never fast enough, or pray enough
It never seems to add up
God, can you meet me in the middle?
I know you are the beginning and the ending of everything
But I need you in between
I struggle with my purpose and personality
I fight with my friends and family
I struggle with my past and my destiny
I know what to do, and I know where I am going
But I often struggle with the in between
God can you meet me in the middle?
In between the faults and the failure
In between the use and the abuse
In between the hurt and the pain
In between the stress and the strain
I am not where I started, but am far from where I want to be
Sometimes it gets rough living in the middle, living in between

My Life

I sacrificed it all; without a cost

I gave up my life and my home

I turned my back on Christ, my eternal father

I gave up everything that matters

For a love, I thought was real, and for a man I thought really loved me

At first it seems that everything was going my way until things took a turn for the worst

It left me hurt, empty, and in total despair

It left me with a hole that nothing or no one could fill

I wanted so much from him, he just couldn't give

I was miserable, frustrated and alone

I gave up, I stopped living, and I still had no plans for leaving

Nobody knows only Jesus Christ

I realized through the testing and the trials God was always by my side

His undeniable love always find me

How did this happen?

How did I get this far? I am so lost and undone

And this, that I thought would kill me

Made me the perfect candidate for his love

In My Moments

My moments of loneliness and desperation leave me in despair
Paralyzed by fear, wondering if you care
I know you are the omniscient and omnipresent
But in these moments I need to know you are there
I need to touch you, feel you, and breathe you
I need to know you care
Problems on every hand, I am without a rescue or a plan
In these moments, where can my soul find refuge?
Where can I find help?
Please do something, do anything, I am desperately pleading!
Throw me a rope I am sinking beneath my load
My moments of pain, are often accompanied by stress and strain
In my struggle to stay alive, if care is not taken, even the TRUTH gets compromised
Life traumatic events have wounded me; they crushed me to the core.
Robbing me of so many things, leaving me in a pool of anger
Now I am bitter inside, what a horrible place to be
Oh Lord, please send help quickly, hurry! Hurry!
I am drowning, almost covered in this pool of sin!

Hope

Don't give up, don't give in
Just when you think it's over
And all seems lost
The pressures of life are caving in
It seems like you are drowning
Jesus won't let you down
He will see you trough
No matter how long it takes
These trials will not kill you
There is more for you than against you
Don't give up, don't give in
Everyone is telling you, "It's over."
Your life is feeling empty
It seems like there is no hope
It appears like you can't win
Don't you give up, don't give in
If you hold on, I know you can win
Jesus won't let you down
He is working it out for you
Just wait and you will see
He will rescue you

My Conscience

My conscience, quiet, and yet so real
My conscience would be telling me
"You shouldn't have; you shouldn't be."
My conscience, lingering in my head
It just won't go away; like the sun on a hot summery day
I tried to deny it
I tried to ignore it
After all, only I can hear it
This constant voice in my head
Just won't leave me, my conscience is pleading with me
I'm tired of drowning it with food, friends and fashion
Ha! Perhaps A trip to the mall might stop it
I tried everything to make this conscience stop
It just won't cease
Not until I'm on bended knees
Total submission is what it needs
I felt uncomfortable; I felt unease
My conscience just keep talking to me
It is my inner voice, and it is trying to guide me
This conscience, this spiritual guidance
This voice is the Holy Spirit at work inside of me
He wants to set me free

The Loud Silence

I am falling, and there is nothing to hold on to

I am reaching out, but there is no one reaching out to me

I am weak, but there is no shoulder to lean on

What am I doing wrong?

So many ears and no one is listening

Everyone is giving pity, but no one is praying

What am I doing wrong? Why can't anyone understand?

Rejected and disappointed by everything and everyone

It's a hard place to be

Set me free from these wounds

That never seems to heal

As the healing process begins, there goes something interrupting

All these wounds are internal, but because of interferences and mishaps

They are surfacing, and they hurt just like in the beginning

The List

Have you ever felt entangled by a list of laws and duties?
A list that you can never satisfy
A list you can't dismiss
The list at work
The list at Church
The list at home
The list that you have created
The list that people gave you
This list of laws requires so much labor
Lord just as I am, you have loved me
Oh! I wish your grace would find me
The list is too long; I need grace to set me free
I have believed a lie, that if I could do just one more thing
Then I will be qualified, and this list would be satisfied
But I've had enough; I will no longer believe this lie
I am trading it for the grace of my Savior
The one who died to destroy these lists!
His last words were; it is finished!

The Struggles

Life is a struggle living in the slum
This way of life seems like it will never be over
Poverty preys on the people like a hungry lion in search for food
Oppression, depression is like a thick cloud hanging over the city
Frustration is the look of every face
Every man for himself, sometimes the hunter becomes the hunted
They will do anything for a piece of bread
What a tragedy, one by one, they lose their dignity
Misery is the order of the day; a hungry man is an angry man.
Crime is on the rampage
As people sell their souls just to live like humans
They do all sorts of things to numb their pain
Imagine children hungry, and there is no food
Potential, talents, brain-wasting away
The only education is how to survive for the day
The harshness of poverty is worse than the punishment for a crime
The crime that they never commit, poverty is the culprit
They struggle to keep their heads above water
Their resistance keeps getting weaker and weaker
As one by one poverty pulls them under
Before you start judging people and point the finger
It is their life, and they are living it; don't be so quick to think
that it was their choice
Some people didn't choose it; it chose them

Acceptance

Why can't you accept me?
I am just another person; that's what I am
I too deserve your time and attention
Why can't I get this job?
Why can't I? I am just as qualified
Why can't you accept me?
Do not disqualify me because of my differences
But celebrate the things we have in common
Everyone is special in their way
God created us to be different
Do not judge anyone because of how they look
If you must make a decision, based it on the content of their character
We have to look beyond our differences
All people are equal
I cry; you cry
I sleep; you sleep
I bleed, and you bleed
You are just like me; we are from the same maker
You are my brother; you are my sister
We are neighbors
I am your children's school teacher
The man that makes your burgers
The firefighter or just a Good Samaritan
That may help you later
I'm not your enemy

Together we can do more for each other.

Let us celebrate each other

Let's get to know one another

There is more to me than what your eyes first see

Why Can't We Get Along?

Why can't we just get along?
Why can't we all live as one?
Why can't we be our brother's keeper?
Why is our love so shallow?
Why do we talk so badly, about each other?
The words from our mouth stings like a bee
Venomous as a viper, killing our brothers and sisters
We should do better; after all we share the same father
And He commands us to love one another
If we do not change, to him we will answer
There is hope for us, but we have to believe it
I don't know about you, but I am ready to fix it
Now is the time to live as one, now is the time to get along
Life is too short; we can't afford to waste another minute
Let's all love each other, no matter what race or gender
Love is the solution, love is the answer

Victim

A victim of circumstances

Imprisoned by my environment

How can I change my way of thinking

If every day I wake up, it's the same type of living

How can I emancipate my mind from a world that's so unkind?

Sometimes I manage to rise above it

Because of God's great power that lives within me

What about you? What about my family?

What about those who can't find this power?

Those who are on the verge of giving up, and giving in

God promises that evil will not triumph over me, Lord help me to believe

Because, on the contrary, there seem to be a few people like me,

That thinks evil has knees because they are always creeping up on me

I can't explain why evil exists, or why it often happen to people who don't deserve it

Nevertheless, one of these beautiful days, God, my God will put an end to this

This very moment, right this minute I have to face it, I have to fight it

My freedom, my faith, my assurance, and my deliverance is in God's hand

What a World

Everybody wants to lead, no one wants to follow

Everyone wants to receive; no one wishes to be the giver

What a selfish world, such a bugger!

Everyone is trying to use somebody deliberately, or unintentionally

There is always some hidden agenda

Everyone wants to survive; everybody wants a ride

We all want to be somebody, and get somewhere

But some people don't want to work; they just want a free ride

That's not fair; how dare you try to use me

There is always a selfish motive, to every charity

If someone was watching us, what would we do differently?

If you take the time to be nice, by just smiling

The result of your returns would be alarming

It doesn't take much to be nice; it takes more to be nasty

It is awful when a smile is too costly

It is sad when you can't say hello to your neighbor

The bus driver or even a stranger

It is terrible when a child does not speak to their mother

Or when a sister does not speak to her brother

Or when a pastor does not speak to a member

These behaviors are ridiculous, this is sin, and we have to do something

What a world to live in

The Issues of My Life

Out of the heart flow the issues of life
The gesticulation of my face bears witness to my pain
My issues are tossing me like waves; I'm neither here nor there
Sometimes I don't even know where I am going
So how will I get there, automatically I become a prey
Danger on the rampage, the devil is out to get me
How can I fight, this enemy?
I see the struggles, I see the strife
But I can't run, there is no place left to hide
Oh, the pain that grips me, the pain that paralyzes me
When I have to deny my children of life essential needs
Two jobs and the only ground I'm covering
Is the one that is beneath my feet.
I have a sick mother who is waiting to be with my dead father
Oh! Don't forget the bill collectors
They have my number!

Pain

Pain is a strain; it stresses the mind and worries the brain

It shattered the heart and weakened the body

This pain is a war, but I can win

It stresses me day out and day in

Release me from your deadly grip!

I will resist this evil with everything in me

I am not your slave; I'm not your prisoner

I will not retreat, I will not surrender

Pain is a thief; pain is a stealer

Creeping up on me, and trying to invade my body

Wait a minute! Stop right there in your tracks!

You have no authority over my body

What gave you this right?

Looting and polluting my body

I've got news for you

Haven't you heard about my FATHER?

I am bought with a price, and I'm set free

From all pains and miseries

Don't you know I can trod, even upon the deadliest of serpents

And it shall by no means hurt me

It is my right, and it is my legacy

Diabetics, Cancers, and all other ailments

Has no place in my body, this is God's property

A Cry for Freedom

Insecurities bound me; it imprisoned me
My burdens and depression shackled me
I thought there was no way out
I was screaming for attention
The silence was so very loud
I felt my innocence slipping away
But my addiction for him was terrifying
These feelings consumed me; I was drowning
I was his slave; I was his servant
Anything for his love, anything for his attention
I was going down into a desperate pit
I wanted an escape; I wanted to get out of it
One day the hands of Jesus touched me
Immediately I was set free
The chains broke
The shackles fell from my knees
I was set free! Free from all the things that used to bind me

Why

If you love me so much, why did you lie?

If I am all you have, then who is that girl on your side?

Why did you make that vow, to take me as your wife?

Why did you swear to love and cherish me?

Making promises, you can't keep

You said you were sorry, but I find it hard to believe

Why do you play with my heart?

Night after night, I am slowly falling apart

Why are you so set on making me cry?

Why do you stay out late at night, acting like a bachelor?

When you know, you have a wife

This life is tiring, and I am disgusted with your lies

Tell me why I should take this from you?

You better start changing, no more excuses!

Rescue Me

I need a rescue; I need a friend
I can't find my way back home
I can't see the path; I don't know where to start,
I have been running far too long in the wrong direction
I need to find rest for my weary legs
I wish I could find a friend, a shoulder, or a hand
Only God can rescue me, in his loving arms I want to be
Rescue me oh Lord!
Save me from this world of insecurities
Come and set me free
I am disliked and deceived
Disappointed, used and abused
Life is more complicated than I thought; it can be rather cruel
No matter what I do,
There is just no breaking through
I need a helping hand
I need a plan; I need salvation
I am in desperate need of a rescue
I need you Lord; I need you to hold my hand

A Stranger in My Home

Mom I am hurting

Can't you see my pain?

Dad I'm so afraid of where I am

Can you kiss away my fears?

Please take away my cares

I am so afraid to talk to you

Every time I try to come close, you are busy with something new

Sometimes I feel if I disappear, you

won't even care

I feel alone, I am like a stranger in my home

I feel ignored, and it seems wrong

I feel neglected and abused

Tell me please, am I of any use?

To this home or this family

Can you just love me? Love me for who I am

Why can't you understand? I need you to love me

Don't let me search for love in all the wrong places

Will you show me that you care?

I am trying, will you meet me half way

Please don't let me go astray

Sometimes I don't understand the things I go through

Mom I need you to tell me that it will be alright; it will be fine

Why do you find me so strange?

Has this ever happened to you?

Why can't you be there for me?

What do you have to lose?

Lord, please help me, help my family
I am down on bended knees
Help us grow in grace
Show us how to love each other, show us how to care
I need a change from this life; it is driving me insane
Please Lord, help me!
I can't face another day
Make it all go away
I just need a change

Sisters

Sisters why do you work so hard to please everyone?

Day in day out, you are busy making yourself be like everyone else

You have a mind of your own, let it shows

And who you are inside is more than what meets the eyes

Everything you see is temporary, so why worry?

Why do you try so hard?

What happen to Miss "I won't let anyone change me!"

You have become everything else, apart from yourself

Now you are frustrated, feeling empty

Who are you now, what have you become?

All caught up in a game of charades

The game is over; take the time to know who you are inside

There is more to you, than fashion and trends

There is more to life than parties and boyfriends

You can't hide, just because you change the color of your hair, skin and eyes

Change from the inside, change your mind and that will show over time

You won't be fulfilled by buying expensive fashions

At the end of the day, you will still be the same

You may think you are on top of your game

But you are not, and that's a fact

So stop flirting with your body, and start making use of your mind

I am not against the way you look; I am on your side

You don't need to do anything; you are perfect the way you are

Live the life God creates for you, and not the one that others build for you

Don't let them influence you

God made you special, and he loves you

Loving Yourself

Don't worry too much about your body
The way you look, the way you shape
Thank God, there are shades of gray
It's not just black and white
There are also the in-betweens, and that's where most of us are
You are not the slimmest, and you are not the biggest
You are not the ugliest, and you are not the prettiest
There are smaller tummies and bigger bellies
Everybody has a brain, use it!
God made us all special
You were created like God, and by God
Don't be fooled by what you hear or see
God knows they have used enough tricks and persuasions
Taking your hard earned money out of your hands
Telling us, they have what it takes for us to look a certain way
Is it worth it? Do not be fooled by their nonsense
I wish they would quit
Finding actors and celebrities
Telling us, we can look like them
Getting us all worked up
Some of us can't help the way we look
We were born to be like this

An Indian will look different from a Caucasian
An African will look different from a Korean
Apples look different from oranges
We all cannot look the same
Accept the beauty of diversity
Enjoy it, love it, live it

We Are Not Objects

Who are you to compare and contrast our body parts, as if we are objects?

With your egotistical self, who told you, that you can use us as you please?

You just wait one minute! Before you start boasting, telling your friends how good you were

We are here for things far greater than just giving you pleasure

Oh! So you think am just being a feminist, am just being factual

I am sick of your oversized ego and the magnitude of your stupidity

Giving us all sorts of name, are you serious, do you even have a brain?

Stop being hooligans, start behaving like human

Whenever you see a lady, another woman, give us the respect we deserve

We are intelligent and strong, after all we are WOMAN!

When you see us, don't judge us base on our skin color

The size of our breast, or by the roundness and firmness of our backsides

Take the time to know us, what's on our mind, try having a conversation

For once in your life, it might help you to see us in a different light

Be respectful, treat us right!

Learn To Be a Man

What makes you believe you are all that?

What makes you think it is all about you?

Why should I give you my attention because you wear the latest brands?

And you appear like you have a few dollars in your pants

What makes you think you deserve me or my time?

I am not galvanized by your beautiful gifts

Are with the games you play

Well, I'm a lot harder to please

It's not always about your needs!

I want! I want! Hold on for a second

What about me?

Caught up in the role of society, with a tunnel vision brain

Cooking, cleaning, and taking care of the family is a woman's place

There is also a role for to play if you manage to take a break

It is not always about you, for once, think about our needs

What have you proven so far, and who are you attempting to please?

Stop playing games with me

Stop being a fool

Be a man, somebody we can count on

Show us you know what it takes, and you can

Make this world a better place

Stop being such a narrow-minded moron!

No Ring, No Bed

Just say no!

Sex is a bi-product of love and relationships

All this sexual energy, you are just burning

Can't wait to give it up

Channel this energy into something productive

Play a sport; get involved in your church or community

Be constructive, whatever your hands find to do, do it with all you might.

Develop your talent; focus on getting a proper education

As my mother would say, "The devil will find work for idle hands".

Listen, if they love you, they will wait

They will do it the right way

Often time's, sex is given in exchange for love

Don't be tricked; they will say "if you like me, then prove it."

There are other ways of showing love, than having sex

Watch a movie in a group

Don't be consumed by this burning

Do not start something you cannot finish

Don't be kissing or petting because it leads to other things

You are setting yourself up, for a major, major fall

Don't you think that it won't happen to you

Don't think you are too smart, even iron, when exposed to heat, will melt

Don't tell yourself, "am in control."

You think you know when to stop?

Once Again, it is a setup, and that's a proven fact

The Ride Through Life

Life is a ride you have to take
Different cars, different ways
It is a journey we all must take
Some choose the fast lane, can't keep up with the speed
Going so fast, Boom! They crashed
And that's the end of their ride on this road of life
Others decide to take their time and smell the roses
A stop or two to take a view
Others may pass them by
Slowly but steadily we will make it to the end of the ride
I will not speed; I'm in no rush to be with my dead family
I will ride on; I will ride slowly
Where they are, I'm in no haste to go
Ride on; ride on, for there are miles and miles to go

Ungrateful

If life is what it is, then accept it?

You are always biting more than you can chew

What is wrong with you, always wanting what others have

Always reaching for more than you need

Your life is not a rehearsal; you can't go back and undo

God has been good to you, stop acting like a fool

I know that somewhere inside you there is enough strength to drop this attitude

What you do not have, won't make you happy

Stop blaming everything and everybody

It is not them; it is you

It is you, quit pointing figures at everybody

Try to see life from a different point of view

Stop being ungrateful, start saying thank you

Start getting involve, live your life for others to see, contribute, be a part of a community

Do something positive, plant a tree

Help a stranger, find a hobby, or donate your time or money to a charity

Have a conversation with a complete stranger

Laugh out loud, dance in the rain, take a trip or a vacation

See how meaningful life can be, if you stop looking at the glass from a half empty position

Making Life Work

I am making life work for me
My life must count for something
I will realize and capitalize on my opportunities
Exhausting all the avenues that lead to my success
I will not stop; I am determined to get the best
I will rise against everything
And everybody that tries to suppress me
I will fight the force of negativity
I will believe the impossible
I will expect the unexpected
Yes, I will, fight the good fight of faith.
I am always expecting a miracle!
The secret to success is to keep on trying
Starting over and over, again; be persistent
Rejected or accepted
Win or lose, pass or fail
There are chances that I must take
I will not settle for mediocrity
I will try and try again because I am destined to succeed
I will focus on my strength while improving my weakness
There will be oppositions; I'm sure
But I will rise above that wind
I will be brave; I will be strong
The enemy will not steal my joy

Kill my dreams, or destroy my talents
For where I am, there is also three other men
God the Father, the Son, and the Holy Spirit
There is only one life to live
I will live my life boldly; I will not shirk back

Failure

I can't fail; it is not a part of my destiny
I will not quit; there is too much to look forward to
I will have success!
I am born to win, I will not give up, and I will not give in
The secret of triumph is trying
I will not fail; there is too much for me to gain
I can't afford to lose; this is not a game
Failure is a state of mind; it takes no doing
I can't fail, unless I stop trying
In order to fail, one has to do nothing
You can only fail when you stop trying
You have to get this; you have to listen
Keep playing it in your head, over and again
Failure can only be present, in the absence of trying

I Am In Love with You

I am in love with you
I can't stop thinking about you
You've got me singing love songs
You've got me smiling all day long

I'm in love with you
I can't eat; I can't sleep
You are all I need
I am missing you like crazy
I can't wait to see you baby
I am in love with you
I am glad the day, "I said I do."
I will leave my castle and join you in your place
As we become one; the season of singing has began
I am happy to share my life with you
I am in love with you

As a lily among thorns so is my darling among men
How bless I am; I am delighted to have your hand
Let me wrap you in my arms, let me enchant you with my charms
My beloved is the apple of my eyes

Then There Was You

I felt like there was no hope for my broken heart
I was so broken, sad, and alone, with no one to call my own
The days I cried, the nights I stayed awake wondering why
My heart was breaking, my soul was longing, and my body was aching
I thought there would be no recovering
Grieving was my friend, and sorrows never leave me
It was immeasurable; there was no end to my misery
Memories of sadness, memories of pain was running around in my head
Playing mental games, trying to turn me insane
Then, there you were, my knight in shining armor
You came and rescued me; your love had healed my broken heart
It set me free, and now I can love again.

My Lover and Friend

I pray your heart and mine will beat together forever
Beat to our song beat as one and beat to the music of love
Melting all the obstacles that keep us apart
Even though we are distant, God has connected our hearts
I never quite understand the fullness of God's plan
But somewhere in there you and I are meant to be
You are everything I need
I remember the day we met, I remember what I said
I remember the look you had on your face
I remember how time and space disappeared
As we lost ourselves in each other eyes
Nothing and no one else matter; this seems like forever
I am experiencing a new kind of happiness
I am yours forever if you let me
I am truly in love with you
You are the one; I know you are the one for me

Good Men

Good men do exist
I married one, and he is a blessing
Watch him grow; watch him stand
He possesses all the qualities of a good man
Rooted and grounded on a firm foundation
Yeah! Good men do exist
Don't listen to the lies, believe what God says
He created them, and they exist
I am passionate about this
I can testify of an excellent man
Saying "I do" was the best plan
I have a husband who loves me
Protects and provides for his family
What a great man!
To God be the glory
I do agree, that they are prodigal sons
Who have lost their purpose and identity
But God will bring them back
God will restore our men
Don't give up on them
Hope do exist
Don't give up on marriages
Don't give up on love

They are created by God, and He loves them
Hence, God can fix it
God can change things, and he can change people.
All things are possible
If you place it in his hand
Watch him change your situation

Mother

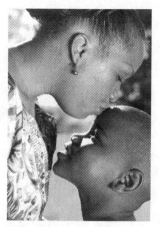

Mother how dear you are to me
You work so hard to make me who I am today
Without a cost, and no pay
You work day and night to give me the best
When it wasn't humanly possible, you went on your knees
Some days I could see the pain on your face
Struggling to get through this very day! But you never gave up
How could one person be so selfless?
You sacrifice so much to give me the best
Bless is my mother!
I am very fortunate to be your daughter
You deserve an award for the life you live, and for the job you did
But no gift could even begin to say how much I appreciate you
God has indeed bless me with a woman like you
I am honored to be your daughter
Mother I love you!

He Has Delivered Me From a Deadly Disease

He has freed me from the crippling effects of what you think of me

Yes I am free from the intimidation of other's opinion

What others think about me, is a vicious disease

It eats away at creativity and individuality.

It feeds on productivity, and often disguise as "if I were you."

People will always have opinions; they are many,

But it will not stop me from becoming all that God has called me to be

I have realized that people will be people

Some may even have a better way to do my duties

I have learnt to not defend my purpose because God alone is your judge

My only defense is love, and it will do more than I can ever say

My deliverance is in effect, and it doesn't matter any longer

I don't have to listen to all these voices; I will not let them build a nest in my head

I know the voice of him, who creates me

He, who have freed me from the opinions of man,

And has given me the ability to walk in my true identity

Fear Doesn't Live Here Anymore

I know who he is

I have let him in through the door

I have treated him as a welcomed guest.

But he doesn't live here anymore

He lived here so long, rent free!

He ate me out slowly

He almost killed me

He took over all the rights to my property

I am glad he doesn't live here anymore

I send him packing, too long; I sat down and did nothing

He is not a friend; he is the enemy

Stealing my joy, and have me wrapped around his thumb like a toy

Having me work for him

Settling for less than I deserved; less than my best

The funniest thing is all this time I was holding on to him. Yes, I was hosting an unwanted guest.

I felt trapped; I was in a wall-less prison.

Little did I know that I had more power than him

The day I found that out, I stopped hosting, and I sent him packing

I Am Nothing Without You

I can't live a day without you

Breathe another breath

Take another step

Without you; without you

I don't want to sing another song

Or dance to the rhythm of my drum

I refuse to do another thing without you

What would it profit me if I become all that I can be without you?

What would I gain, other than a name, if I traveled the world by land, air, and sea?

What is left to do, after I have met with the mighty, and lavishly indulged in my wildest fantasy?

What would all this profit me; if I have no connection to the one who created me?

How empty I would feel to have enjoyed all that royalty without ever meeting my majesty

God has given his life, so that I can live abundantly.

I thought long and hard; I have tallied the cost

Now here I stand with all my reasons why, and they still can't justify a life without you.

Without you; without you

There is no me without you

No peace without you

No joy without you

Purposeful living begins with you

Unsatisfied

I can never get enough of him

Every minute spent with him is electrifying

I am intoxicated by his love

I am enraptured, magnetized by his presence

Overtaken by his unrelenting pursuit

I surrender all that I am to you

I want to immerse myself in him

I am just not satisfied, he keeps me wanting more

I have developed such an insatiable appetite

I desire him more than the pleasures of life

The love that I have for him, I can't even begin to describe

I do not want a relief from this feeling

It gives me a sense of completeness, abundance, and acceptance

The joy I have from being with him, lacks nothing

It is so freeing to be with him, time has no meaning

My soul desires to be with him

My heart longs for him more that the field longs for rain

Only he can satisfy my longing

Only he can fill me up

I Need You

I need you, and you need me

He created us like this

We need each other

Together we can get more done

Together we are a part of a community, a family

Apart we are an easier target for the enemy

Who thrives on creating disunity

He divides and destroys

He knows the power we have when we work together

I need you my sister; I need you my brother

He hates family, so he lies in order to sow enmity

He is a serpent; that has led us to believe that we do not need anybody

We are created to do great works as a body

We need to build each other up

We need to demonstrate love and support for our brothers and sisters

We need to build an environment that celebrate each other

Rather than resenting one another

Stop competing with each other; we are children of the same father

We are all gifted in different areas, and when we come together, we can do wonders

I need you, and you need me

I am here to help you grow, and you are here to help me improve

We should strive to live in love with each other.

God I Need You

I need you in my life all day

I need to have you every minute of the day

I need you at my strongest and my weakest

I need to have you close to me

I need to have you at the center of all I do

I need to spend time basking in your presence

Worshiping with my heart; hosting your Holy Spirit, which gives me pure joy

I need you to teach me your ways, show me how to please you

I need you here with me, holding my hands and guiding my steps

Take me to your dwelling place, and show me the meaning of grace

Unveil the beauty of your glory, and decode the mysteries of your plans

I need you to give me the keys to your throne room so that I can visit every day

I don't just want to visit; my desire is to stay

I need to live in your presence

Each and every day

Take it all Away

Take it all away; take away my pride
Take away the urge to sin, and kill the appetite
Save me from myself; save me completely from
Self-righteousness, Self-indulgent, Selfishness, Self-centeredness
Kill my flesh, and deliver me from this Cane mentality
This attitude of competing and comparing my gifts
Take away the list; take away performance
Let me come into your presence with empty hands
There is nothing I can give, to you it belongs
Everything thing I have, you gave me
Naked I came into this world, and everything I have, I will leave
How dear I think that I have earned this
My self-righteousness is causing a stench
Take away the lines that I have drawn, and the unforgiveness
that comes with it
I am drowning in my self-centeredness; my biggest enemy is me
Take away this self-proclaim, Self-made identity that I have created
Strip me of me; I surrender all to you

I am living for him

I was never created to live an ordinary life
I am living for an extra-ordinary God

He is multifaceted, and he created me special for him
He has given me many gifts and talents
I use them all to praise him, which often leave people wondering
People have judged me; labeled me

They have discouraged me; in telling I am too busy
It's hard for them to understand because they did not make me
I have even hidden my blessing, my gifts, as a way to fit in
But God often take me back to the Parable of the Talents
People have told me I will burn out because I use all my gifts
to praise him
They often try to narrow me down to one thing
Lord let me be like the burning bush, that burns, but not burnout
It doesn't matter what they do; I am determined to live for you